LIFE CYCLES
Worms

by Robin Nelson

first step nonfiction

Lerner Publications Company · Minneapolis

Look at the worm.

Look at all the worms.

A worm is an animal that lives in the **soil**.

How does a worm grow?

A worm starts as an egg
inside a tiny **cocoon**.

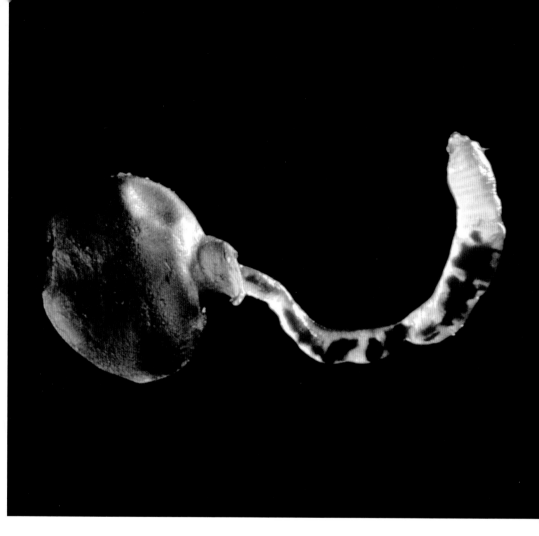

The worm **hatches.**

The baby worm is thin and white.

Worms do not have eyes
or ears.

But worms have a mouth.

Worms eat dirt.

Worms eat plants.

They grow bigger and longer.

Worms make **burrows** in the ground.

They need to stay cool
and wet.

This worm is grown up.

It is fun to watch worms.

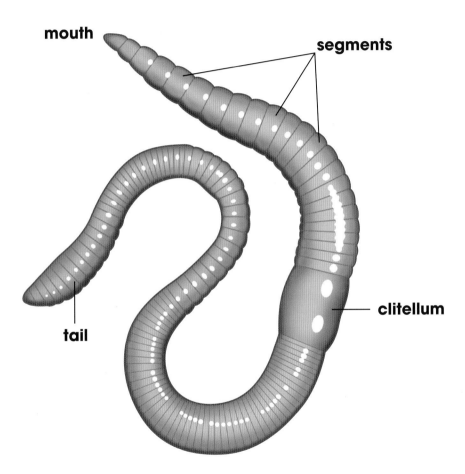

mouth

segments

clitellum

tail

Adult Worms

The body of a worm is made out of many segments. One segment, the clitellum, makes a cocoon for worm eggs.

Worms lay eggs in the spring and fall. The summer can be too hot and dry. In the winter, they tunnel very deep into the ground and stay there. In the spring, they come out again and a new worm life cycle begins.

Worm Facts

 Worms are very helpful to the earth. Their tunnels help keep the soil healthy.

 A worm will not die if a bird breaks off the worm's head or tail. It will grow a new head or tail!

 Worms, especially night crawlers, usually only come out at night.

 Why do worms come out when it rains? The soil is too wet, and their tunnels are flooded.

Many kinds of animals eat worms. In some parts of the world, even people eat worms!

 The body of a grown-up worm has 120 to 170 segments.

 Worms have small hairs on their bodies to help them move.

Worms have five hearts.

Glossary

 burrows – tunnels

 cocoon – a sack or shell that protects the worm eggs

 hatches – comes out of an egg

 soil – dirt

Index

The images in this book are used with the permission of: © iStockphoto.com/Viorika Prikhodko, front cover; © Dwight R. Kuhn, pp. 2, 3, 6, 7, 10, 14, 15, 22 (top three images); © Paul Debois/ GAP Photos/Getty Images, pp. 4, 22 (bottom); © iStockphoto.com/Rainbowphoto, p. 5; © iStockphoto.com/Pattie Calfy, p. 8; © London Scientific Films/Oxford Scientific/Photolibrary, p. 9; © Nigel Cattlin/Visuals Unlimited, p. 11; © Kathie Atkinson/Oxford Scientific/ Jupiterimages, p. 12; © Konrad Wothe/Minden Pictures/Getty Images, p. 13; © Paul Debois/ Gap Photo/Visuals Unlimited, p. 16; © Matthias Tunger/Photonica/Getty Images, p. 17; © Laura Westlund/Independent Picture Service, pp. 18, 20, 21.

Lerner Publications Company
A division of Lerner Publishing Group, Inc.
241 First Avenue North
Minneapolis, MN 55401 U.S.A.

Website address: www.lernerbooks.com

Library of Congress Cataloging-in-Publication Data

Nelson, Robin.
    Worms / by Robin Nelson.
        p.   cm. — (First step nonfiction. Animal life cycles)
    ISBN: 978–0–7613–4064–5 (lib. bdg. : alk. paper)
    1. Worms—Juvenile literature. I. Title.
QL386.6.N45 2009
592'.3—dc22   2008029472

Manufactured in the United States of America
1 2 3 4 5 6 – DP – 14 13 12 11 10 09